Nutrition recommendations during TCM - Spleen - heat and moisture infects the spleen

Please check these recommendations always with a nutrition consultant, therapist, doctor or dietician. The recipes and the list of ingredients are supporting the conventional medical therapy. The calorie disclosures of fresh ingredients (fruit and vegetables) vary according to quality and time of harvest. The contents were checked by a dietician and a nutrition consultant for the Traditional Chinese Medicine (TCM).

Author:
©2020 Josef Miligui
www.ebns.at

AF285136

Source:
The lists are created from the EBNS database for nutritional counseling. The database is used by dietitians, therapists and doctors for advising the patient / client.

Literature:
The specialist literature and the training documents of the German and Austrian dietary and traditional Chinese medicine serve as a knowledge base. We have used the documents as a basis of knowledge, adapted it to our experience and completed them.
http://nutribook.info/

Production and publishing:
BoD – Books on Demand, Norderstedt
ISBN: 9783752894066

Nutrition recommendations for TCM - Spleen - heat and moisture infects the spleen

1 Treatment strategy

Build Qi, drain moisture, cool heat, drain moisture.
Hot NO, warm-little, neutral YES, refreshing and cold little, sour NO

2 Avoid

Tropical fruits, raw vegetables, dairy products, wheat, white flour, sweets, alcohol, coffee, smoking, fat-sweet, fat-salty, fried, baked, smoked meat fried and grilled, garlic, onion, hot and hot spices.

3 Breakfast

	kkal. per serving
Barley water	44
Cardamom water	16
Cooling rice dish with grapefruit	234
Legumes	31
Rice porridge with orange peel	119
Rice porridge with shrubs (seeds) Yi Yi Ren	211,5
Tea from Maidis stigma	0
Tea from rosemary	1
Tea from sage	4

4 Snack

Adzuki Bean and Rice Soup	199

5 Lunch

8 treasures of rice	212
Barley water	44
Cardamom water	16
Cooling rice dish with grapefruit	234
Indian Dal soup	255
Legumes	31
Rice porridge with orange peel	119
Rice porridge with shrubs (seeds) Yi Yi Ren	211,5
Tea from Maidis stigma	0
Tea from rosemary	1
Tea from thyme	0

6 Afternoon

n.a.

7 Dinner

8 Any time

9 Recipes

(rec.) = You can use more.
(little) = You should use less than specified
(omit) = omit.

9.1 8 treasures of rice

Strengthens kidney and bladder, builds up Qi, strengthens the spleen, repels moisture, reduces internal heat, prevents cancer, builds heart, calms nerves.
Cooking time approx. 1 hour
Calories p. portion: 212
4 portions

Quantity of ingredients
Lily bulbs 1 table spoon / 5g. () - cool - sweet, bitter .... *
Longane 1 table spoon / 5g. (little) - warm - sweet.. *
King Solomon's-seal 1 table spoon / 5g. () - neutral - sweet, bitter .... *
Yam root, yam root tuber 1 table spoon / 5g. () - neutral - sweet .... *
Coix (seeds) YiYi Ren 1 table spoon / 5g. (rec.) - cool - sweet, neutral .... *
Rice wild (nature rice) 1 1/2 cups / 240g. (rec.) - neutral - sweet, bitter .... metal
Water 8-10 cups / 800g. (yes) - cool - salty..earth

Cooking instructions:
Each one 1 tbsp: Bai He, Longan, Yu Zhu, Da Zao, Shan Yao, Lian Mi, Yi Yi Ren, Qian Shi
Add hot water and soak for about 30 minutes. Then add 1 - 2 cups of rice (normal) and simmer for 1/2 to 1 hour until the rice is very soft. Or: Cook for about 3 hours with the herbs a congee. Then the herbs do not have to be soaked.

9.2 Adzuki Bean and Rice Soup

Reduces moisture, directs down, reduces gastrointestinal heat, builds up essence, strengthens muscles after heat illness, builds up body fluids.
Cooking time approx. 2 hours
Calories p. portion: 199
1 portions

Quantity of ingredients
Adzuki beans 8 table spoons / 40g. (rec.) - neutral - sweet, sour.............water
Rice round grain 2 table spoons / 20g. (rec.) - neutral - sweet.................metal
Water 1 1/2 cups / 200g. (yes) - cool - salty..earth
Honey 1 table spoon / 8g. () - cold - sweet...earth

Cooking instructions:
Boil soaked adzuki beans and round grain rice in a ratio of 4: 1 in water until a thin pulb has formed. Sweet as needed; possibly puree.

Effect: This recipe strengthens kidney, spleen and stomach and is particularly suitable for mothers with too little milk flow.

9.3   Barley water

Moisturizes the lungs and large intestine, forces spleen, cools bladder, moisturizes intestines, relaxes, builds up Qi, spreads, forces spleen, passes downwardly.
Cooking time approx. 2 hours
Calories p. portion: 44
10 portions
Allergens: A

Quantity of ingredients
Barley 1/4 lbs - 4oz / 100g. (rec.) - cool - sweet, little salty ....earth
Water 8 cup - 1/2 1 Gallone / 1900g. (yes) - cool - salty ....earth
Lemon peel 1 knife tip / 1g. (rec.) - cool - bitter..fire
Cinnamon ground 1 pinch / 1g. () - hot - acrid, sweet ....*
Fig 4-5 pieces / 100g. (yes) - warm - sweet ....earth
Ginger fresh 1 pinch / 1g. (yes) - warm - acrid ....metal
Clove 1 piece / 0,5g. (little) - warm - acrid..metal
Salt 1 pinch / 1g. (yes) - cold - salty ....water
Cocoa 1 pinch / 1g. () - warm - sweet, bitter..fire

Cooking instructions:
Give the barley in a pot of 2 l. water and let it swell for 5 hours. Then heat the barley, add the fig, cinnamon, clove, ginger and salt. Simmer for 2 hours and strain the hot barley water. Add the grated lemon peel and cocoa.

9.4   Cardamom water

Warms the middle, dissolves stagnation, directs upwards. Tonifies the kidney-Yang, nourishes bones and tendons, warms kidneys and spleen, forces stomach, dissolves flatulence, contracts, controls excessive urination, helps with digestive weakness.
Cooking time approx. 20 min
Calories p. portion: 16
4 portions

Quantity of ingredients
Cardamom 2 table spoons / 18g. () - warm - acrid .... *
Water 4 cup / 1000g. (yes) - cool - salty...earth

Cooking instructions:
Finely crush cardamom pods in a mortar. Boil with 1 liter of water and cook gently for 10 minutes over medium heat. Fill cardamom water through a sieve in glasses and serve hot.

9.5   Cooling rice dish with grapefruit

Lowers lung Qi, nourishes fluids, dissolves mucus, dries out, passes downwardly, warms the stomach and spleen, harmonizes the intestine, forces Qi, reduces moisture, strengthens Qi and Kidney Jing, moisturizes, relaxes, builds up Qi, spreads.
Cooking time approx. 20 min
Calories p. portion: 234
4 portions
Allergens: GHO

Quantity of ingredients
Rice round grain 1 cup / 120g. (rec.) - neutral - sweet ....metal
Water 5 cups / 600g. (yes) - cool - salty...earth
Hazelnuts 2 table spoons / 20g. (yes) - neutral - sweet ....earth
Raisins 2 table spoons / 20g. (little) - warm - sweet..................................earth
Agave nectar 1 table spoon / 10g. () - cool - sweet.. *
Salt 1 pinch / 0,2g. (yes) - cold - salty ....water
Almond puree 1 table spoon / 10g. (little) - neutral - sweet ....earth
Grapefruit (Pomelo) 1 piece / 200g. (rec.) - cool - sweet, sour....................fire
Butter organic 2 teaspoons / 20g. (yes) - neutral - sweet...........................earth

Cooking instructions:
Preparation on the eve: Pour round grain rice into cold water and cook.
Soak chopped hazelnuts and raisins in some hot water overnight.

In the morning: Stir in a little hot water some agave syrup; add the rice
and heat; add a small pinch of salt, almond paste, chopped grapefruit,
the soaked chopped hazelnuts and raisins and mix; Serve with a small
piece of butter.

9.6   Indian Dal soup

Reduces internal heat and moisture, softens, passes downwardly,
strengthens spleen and liver, regulates Qi flow, moisturizes, relaxes,
builds up Qi, spreads, forces liver and kidney, reduces damp heat.
Cooking time approx. 30 min
Calories p. portion: 256
2 portions
Allergens: EN

Quantity of ingredients
Lentils 3/8 lbs - 6oz / 175g. (little) - neutral - sweet, sour .... water
Sesame oil 3 table spoons / 30g. (little) - cool - sweet .... earth
Carrot 1 piece / 100g. (rec.) - neutral - sweet .... earth
Onion (shallot) 1 piece / 15g. () - warm - acrid, sweet .... metal
Water 1 1/2 cups / 200g. (yes) - cool - salty .... earth
Ginger fresh 2 slices / 1g. (yes) - warm - acrid .... metal
Salt 1 pinch / 0,5g. (yes) - cold - salty .... water
Soy sauce 1 teaspoon / 3g. (little) - cold - salty .... water
Parsley 1 teaspoon (chopped) / 3g. (yes) - warm - bitter .... wood
Thyme 1 teaspoon / 3g. (rec.) - warm - bitter .... *
Basil 1 table spoon / 5g. (rec.) - warm - acrid, bitter .... fire

Cooking instructions:
Soak the lentils overnight.
in a hot pot, carrot, onion and a little ginger fry, pour water. Add the
lentils and cook until soft. Add salt or soy sauce and cook for another 10
minutes.
Stir in parsley before serving; Sprinkle thyme or basil over it.
Variant: Other herbs such as sage, rosemary or lovage allow a variety
of flavors.

9.7 Legumes

Strengthens spleen and liver, regulates Qi flow, moisturizes, relaxes, builds up Qi, spreads, nourishes blood and Qi, diuretic, harmonizes Qi (in the middle and lower heater), detoxifies, reduces internal heat and moisture.
Cooking time approx. 30 min
Calories p. portion: 31
5 portions

Quantity of ingredients
Pinto beans speckled 1/4 lbs - 4oz / 100g. (little) - neutral - sweet .... water
Lentils 1/8 lbs - 2oz / 50g. (little) - neutral - sweet, sour .... water
Peas, green 1/8 lbs - 2oz / 50g. (yes) - neutral - sweet .... water
Water 4 cup / 1000g. (yes) - cool - salty .... earth
Lemon 1 slice / 2g. () - cold - sour .... wood
Juniper berry 6 pieces / 2g. (little) - warm - sweet, acrid, bitter .... fire
Thyme 1 Twig / 3g. (rec.) - warm - bitter .... *
Rosemary 1 Twig / 3g. (rec.) - warm - bitter .... fire
Carrot 1 piece / 100g. (rec.) - neutral - sweet .... earth
Savory 1-2 teaspoons / 5g. (rec.) - warm - bitter .... water
Ginger fresh a great piece / 3g. (yes) - warm - acrid .... metal
Bay leaf 2-3 leaves / 1g. () - warm - acrid .... *
Wakame 1-2 strips / 1g. (little) - cold - salty .... water

Cooking instructions:
Legumes such as beans, lentils, peas or chickpeas are soaked in plenty of cold water for several hours to three days. The water should be changed every 8 hours. Then pour off soaking water and wash legumes thoroughly.

Preparation:
Cook the legumes with fresh cold water and a slice of ginger and bring to froth. Cook without lid for about 5 minutes, scooping off the foam. Only then add the following ingredients: a slice of lemon or lemon juice, crush juniper berries, thyme; (possibly 1 knife tip of asafoetida in case of severe indigestion). Add savory, sage, juniper, fenugreek seeds, carrots, bay leaves, fresh ginger, wakame algae.

Simmer on the slightest flame until beans or lentils have the desired consistency.
This base can be stored for 3-4 days in the refrigerator.

9.8 Rice porridge with orange peel

Warms the stomach and spleen, harmonizes the intestine, forces Qi, reduces moisture. brings the Liver Qi in motion, cools heat, moisturizes, relaxes, builds up Qi, spreads. nourishes blood, moisturizes, relaxes, builds up Qi, spreads.
Cooking time approx. 10 min
Calories p. portion: 120
4 portions
Allergens: L

Quantity of ingredients
Rice variety any 1 cup / 100g. (rec.) - warm - sweet .... metal
Water 6 cups / 600g. (yes) - cool - salty .... earth
Olive oil 1 table spoon / 10g. (little) - cool - sweet .... earth
Champignon 1/2 cup / 50g. (rec.) - cool - sweet .... earth
Celery sticks 1/2 bunch / 60g. (rec.) - cool - sweet .... earth
Basic recipe for a chicken soup (warming) 3-4 table spoons / 40g. () - warm - **
Salt 1 pinch / 0,5g. (yes) - cold - salty .... water

Cooking instructions:
The day before boil the rice with the orange peel and water in a ratio of about 1: 6. The amount of water determines the thickness of the mash (pure matter of taste). Put the rice in a saucepan with good insulation and a heavy lid. It is important to simmer the rice after a short boil on the slightest flame, otherwise it burns. Boil the rice for 2-4 hours. The longer he cooks, the more he strengthens. Heat the oil in a saucepan, add the chopped champignon and celery and sauté briefly. Add the rice. Add vegetable broth or water, warm up, salt.

9.9 Rice porridge with shrubs (seeds) Yi Yi Ren

Warms stomach, harmonizes the intestine, forces Qi, reduces moisture, forces spleen, nourishes and forces Lunge, reduces internal heat, moves Qi and blood, diuretic, cools in internal heat.
Cooking time approx. 25 min
Calories p. portion: 212
2 portions

Quantity of ingredients
Water 4 cups / 450g. (yes) - cool - salty .... earth
Rice variety any 1 cup / 120g. (rec.) - warm - sweet .... metal
Lemon peel 1/4 piece / 2g. (rec.) - cool - bitter .... fire
Coix (seeds) YiYi Ren 1/2 cup / 50g. (rec.) - cool - sweet, neutral .... *
Cress 1 table spoon / 6g. (rec.) - cool - sweet .... metal

Cooking instructions:
Cook rice porridge according to basic recipe with a half cup of Yi Yi Ren and lemon peel. Simmer for 1 hour and then sprinkle cress over it.

9.10 Tea from celery sticks

Brings the Liver Qi in motion, cools heat, moisturizes, relaxes, builds up Qi, spreads.
Cooking time approx. 15 min
Calories p. portion: 1
4 portions
Allergens: L

Quantity of ingredients
Celery sticks 2 table spoons (chopped) / 18g. (rec.) - cool - sweet ....earth
Water 2 cup / 500g. (yes) - cool - salty..earth

Cooking instructions:
Heat the water till it boils and put it aside. Add cutted celery and cook for 10 min. to let go. Strain. Sweet to taste with honey.

9.11 Tea from rosemary

Dries out, passes downwardly, forces heart, lung and spleen Qi, forces liver-blood, forces heart-Yin, expels spleen heat / cold moisture, strengthens spleen and kidney Yang.
Cooking time approx. 15 min
Calories p. portion: 1
4 portions

Quantity of ingredients
Rosemary 2-4 teaspoons / 6g. (rec.) - warm - bitter......................................fire
Water 2 cup / 500g. (yes) - cool - salty..earth

Cooking instructions:
Heat the water till it boils and put it aside. Add rosemary and 10 min. to let go. Strain. Sweet to taste with honey.
Afternoon Food

9.12 Tea from sage

Distributes mucus, passes downwardly, activates Wei Qi, forces Qi.
Cooking time approx. 15 min
Calories p. portion: 4
4 portions

Quantity of ingredients
Sage 2 teaspoons / 6g. (rec.) - neutral - bitter, spicy....................................fire
Water 2 cup / 500g. (yes) - cool - salty...earth

Cooking instructions:
Heat the water till it boils and put it aside. Add sage and 10 min. to let go. Strain. Sweet to taste with honey.

9.13 Tea from thyme

Converts mucus, forces lungs and spleen, dries out, passes downwardly.
Cooking time approx. 10 min
Calories p. portion: 0
4 portions

Quantity of ingredients
Thyme 3 table spoons / 6g. (rec.) - warm - bitter.. *
Water 2 cup water / 500g. (yes) - cool - salty ....earth

Cooking instructions:
Heat the water till it boils and put it aside. Add thyme and 10 min. to let go. Strain. Sweet to taste with honey.
Drink 2 to 3 cups daily by mouth

10 Effects of food

10.1 Use ingredients: recommendable

Adzuki beans
Amaranth
Artichoke
Asparagus (green or white)
Balm
Barley
Barley not peeled
Basic recipe for a fish soup
Basic recipe for a rice soup (Congee)
Basic recipe for a vegetable soup
(nutritious)
Basil
Basil (fresh)
Bitter orange peel
Carrot
Carrot (Early Carrot)
Carrot juice without sugar
Celery sticks
Champignon
Chenpi (chinese tangerine bowl)
Chervil
Chinese cabbage
Coix (seeds) YiYi Ren
Coriander
Corn silk tea
Cress
Dandelion juice
Endive salad
Grapefruit (Pomelo)
Grapefruit dried peel
Grapefruit juice
Green tea
Herbs bitter
Herbs wild
Hyssop
Kohlrabi

Leaf salads (bitter)
Lemon peel
Lettuce
Marjoram
Millet
Millet flakes
Miso
Mung bean
Oregano dried
Pearl barley
Peppermint
Radicchio
Radish
Radish horseradish
Reishi mushroom
Rice (fragrance)
Rice (whole grain)
Rice Basmati
Rice black
Rice flour
Rice long grain rice
Rice red
Rice round grain
Rice sweet
Rice variety any
Rice wild (nature rice)
Rosemary
Rye
Rye flour
Sage
Savory
Soybeans, yellow
Thyme
Tsampa (roasted barley flour)
Wormwood

10.2 Use ingredients: yes

Bitter melon
Black tea
Boletus mushroom
Butter organic
Carp
Celery root
Chanterelle

Chicken egg
Chicken stomach
Coconut flakes
Coconut grated
Corn
Crucian
Fig

Fig dried
Fish pieces mixed (fresh water)
Ginger fresh
Gourd
Grape juice red
Grape juice white
Ground
Ground caraway
Hazelnuts
Herbs various
Iceberg lettuce
Lentils black
Lentils red
Malt
Morel (black, dried)
Morel, dried
Multi-grain bread (gray bread)
Octopus
Olives
Parsley
Parsley root
Parsnip
Peanut oil
Peanuts
Peas
Peas, green
Perch

Pigeon
Pine nuts
Pistachios
Potato
Pumpkin seeds
Quinoa
Radish black
Rapeseed oil
Rice noodles
Saffron
Salmon
Salt
Shark
Shiitake, dried
Soy Tofu
Soybeans, black
Sunflower seeds
Sweet potato
Trout
Umeboshi plums (Japanese apricots)
Vanilla
Vanilla powder
Water
Water hot
White bread (wheat bread)
Zucchini

10.3 Use ingredients: little

Agar agar (kelp)
Almond marzipan
Almond milk
Almond puree
Anchovy / Sardine
Anise (Common Fennel)
Apple (sour)
Apple (sweet)
Apple juice (natural cloudy)
Apricot
Apricots
Arrowroot
Aubergine
Avocado
Bamboo shoots
Bean oil
Beef bone marrow
Beef fillet
Beef heart
Beef kidney
Beef liver
Beef lungs (calf)
Beef meat
Beef meat (calf)

Beef meatbones
Beef stomach
Beer (Pils)
Beer (Top-fermented German dark beer)
Black beans
Blackberry´s
Black-eyed peas
Blueberry
Blueberry juice
Boxhorn clover seeds
Breadcrumbs (wheat bread, bread roll)
Broad beans (thick beans)
Broccoli
Brussels sprouts
Buckwheat
Burdock root tea
Bush beans
Butter beans white
Buttermilk
Calamari
Cashews
Cauliflower
Caviar

Cereal coffee
Chard
Chestnuts
Chicken liver
Chicken meat
Chickpeas
Chicory
Chives
Chlorella (fresh water)
Clementines
Clove
Coconut milk
Corn Grease (Polenta)
Crab
Cranberry
Cranberry juice
Cream, sweet 30%
Cumin (Caraway seed)
Curcuma
Curd cheese 20%
Curd cheese 40%
Dandelion (young plants)
Dandelionroots tea
Dates dried
Deer meat
Dill
Duck (heart)
Duck (slaughtered)
Eel
Elderberry blossom tee
Fennel
Fennel tea
Feta cheese
French beans
Goat cheese
Goose
Goose egg
Goose parts
Gooseberry
Grapes red
Grapes white
Grass carp
Herring
Juniper berry
Kefir
Kidney beans (red)
Kombu seaweed (Saccharina japonica)
Lamb bones
Lamb meat
Lamb shoulder
Lamb's lettuce
Leek
Lentils
Lentils yellow

Lima beans
Longane
Lovage
Lychee
Lychee in Preserved
Mallow (Malva sylvestris) blossom tea
Margarine
Margarine (diet)
Mediterranean fish (cod, plaice,
haddock, sea eel, mackerel)
Miso paste (soy bean paste)
Mullet
Mussels
Mustard seeds
Oat flakes (whole grain)
Oat flour
Oat fusion (baby food)
Oat meal
Okra
Olive oil
Oyster mushroom
Pear
Pear juice
Pepper Cayenne
Pepper white (ground)
Peppercorns
Peppers
Peppers (rose peppers)
Pheasant
Pinto beans speckled
Plaice
Pork heart
Pork knuckle
Pork liver
Pork meat
Pork skin
Pork stomach
Pumpkin
Pumpkin seed oil
Quail
Quail egg
Quince
Rabbit liver
Rabbit meat
Raisins
Raspberry
Raspberry dried (immature)
Red cabbage
Rice malt
Romaine lettuce / lettuce salad
Sago (cereals)
Sake
Salsify
Sauerkraut (cutted cabbage fermented)

Savoy cabbage / kale
Seacrab
Sesame oil
Shrimp
Sour cherries
Sour cream 15% fat
Sour milk
Sour milk cheese 20%
Soy sauce
Soybean milk
Soybean oil
Spinach
Spiny lobsters
Star anise
Strawberries

Strawberry Juice
Sunflower oil
Tangerine
Tarragon (Estragon)
Tuna
Turkey breast meat
Turmeric (yellow root)
Vegetable juice
Wakame
Walnuts
Watermelon
Wheat germ oil
White beans
White cabbage
Yarrow tea

10.4 Do not use contra-acting foods

Banana
Banana (cooking banana)
Berry juice
Bulgur (cereals)
Cantaloupe
Carambola (Star fruit)
Cherry
Cherry juice
Chili (pod or ground)
Cinnamon ground
Cinnamon sticks
Cocoa
Cod
Coffee
Couscous
Cow's milk (1.5% fat)
Cow's milk (whole milk 3.5% fat)
Cucumber
Currant (black)
Currant (red)
Currant (white)
Curry
Deer meat
Fresh cheese
Fruit tea
Garlic
Ginger powder
Goat
Goat and sheep's milk
Green spelt
Hawthorn
Hibiscus tea
Honey
Kiwi
Kumquats
Lemon

Lemon juice
Lime
Lobster
Mango
Maple syrup
Mineral water
Mold cheese
Mozzarella
Mulberry fruit
Mung bean sprouting
Mutton
Mutton
Nutmeg
Oat
Onion (shallot)
Onion (spring onion)
Onion read
Onion white
Orange
Orange juice
Oysters
Papaya
Parmesan
Peaches
Peaches (canned)
Pimento
Pineapple
Pineapple (from a can)
Pineapple juice without sugar
Plum
Pomegranate
Rabbit
Radish (white, green, purple-red)
Red wine
Rhubarb
Rose hip

Rose hip tea
Sorrel
Spelled (Dark) bread
Spelled grain
Spelled semolina
Spelled wholemeal flour
Spirit
Sugar brown
Sugar candy white
Sugar cane sugar
Sugar fructose - fruit sugar
Sugar glucose - grapes sugar
Sugar Milk Sugar
Sugar molasses
Sugar white
Tomato

Vinegar (Apple vinegar)
Vinegar (Red wine vinegar)
Vinegar Aceto Balsamico
Wheat
Wheat beer
Wheat bran
Wheat bulgur
Wheat flakes
Wheat flour
Wheat semolina
Wheat semolina for children
White wine
Wild boar meat
Yogi tea
Yogurt (natural, 1.5% fat)
Yogurt (natural, 3.5% fat)

11 Complementary

11.1 Mint

Mentha arvensis
Preparation: Healing tea (infusion)
Eliminates internal heat, dispels wind-heat.
Pour 2-4 g with 250 ml of boiling water and let stand for 10 minutes. Then sieve. Drink in a single dose on an empty stomach.
Casting: Pour 1 g of powder with hot water, leave to simmer and then drink on an empty stomach, possibly sweeten the tea with a little honey;
Ointment: mix some mint powder with yellow vaseline, almond oil, lanolin or other fat base; then apply the cooling and soothing ointment to the head, chest, abdomen or other hot, painful, jammed or inflamed parts of the body.
Do not use on: severe shivering, nervous exhaustion.

11.2 Sorrel

Rumex crispus, rad. / Rumex acetosa herb.
Preparation: Different effects
Eliminates moisture-heat, dissipates heat-toxins, regulates liver-qi and intestinal-qi, dissipates wind-cold and heat-wetness.
Pour fresh or dried leaves with water and leave to soak for at least ten minutes.
Do not use during pregnancy and lactation.

12 Basics of Nutrition

The basic principles of nutrition described herein are general recommendations. They are not aimed at a specific form of therapy. Recommendations concerning a therapy have priority.

12.1 Nutrition

Regular meals in a relaxed atmosphere. A warm breakfast is considered a good start into the day.

The main meals ought to be taken for lunch – supper in the early evening. Pay attention to feeling hungry or sated: don't eat too much nor remain hungry is the rule

Prepare the meals freshly from natural, regional products. Frozen, heat-conserved, industrially prepared or foodstuffs cooked in the microwave oven are rejected.

Choice of foodstuffs according to the season: more cooling food in summer, more warming food in winter.

Eat cooked food at least twice a day. Food and drinks ought to be lukewarm, never ice-cold or hot.

Raw vegetables, briefly cooked vegetables, freshly squeezed juices and mineral water are not recommended. Milk and dairy products are only included in the diet if they don't cause problems. Don't use therapeutic recipes over a longer period without consulting your doctor or therapist.

Varied food

Enjoy the diversity of foodstuffs. Characteristics of a balanced nutrition are variety, suitable combination and a balanced quantity of rich and low energy foodstuffs (on one hand avoiding undersupply with essential nutrients and on the other hand to take to many undesirable substances).

A lot of Cereal Products - and Potatoes

Bread, pasta, rice, cereal flakes (best wholemeal) as well as potatoes contain almost no fat, but many vitamins, mineral nutrients, trace elements, roughage and secondary plant substances. These foodstuffs ought to be taken with low-fat side dishes.

Vegetables and Fruit – „Take Five" every day ... 5 portions of vegetables and fruit a day, as fresh as possible, briefly cooked, or maybe one portion as a juice – ideal as a side dish to every meal as well as snack between meals: Thus a lot of vitamins, mineral nutrients as well as roughage and secondary plant substances

Daily milk and dairy products
Milk and Dairy Products every Day, once or twice per Week Fish; meat, sausages as well as eggs moderately. These foodstuffs contain valuable nutrients like calcium in the milk, iodine selenium and omega-3 fat acids in saltwater fish. Meat is favorable due to its high content of disposable iron and the vitamins B1, B6 and B12. Quantities of 300 – 600 g meat and sausage per week are sufficient. Prefer low-fat products, especially in meat- and dairy products.

Low-fat and fatty Foodstuffs
Fat supplies us with essential fat acids and fatty foodstuffs contain also fat-soluble vitamins. Fat is high in energy; therefore much fat in the food may cause overweight, possibly also cancer. Too many saturated fat acids may further a tendency for cardio-vascular diseases in the long term. Prefer vegetable oils and fats (e.g. rapeseed-, olive-, soya-oils and solid fats produced therefrom). Beware of invisible fat in meat- and dairy products, pastry and sweets as well as in fast-food and convenience foods. 70 – 90 g fat per day is sufficient.

Moderately Sugar and Salt
Take sugar and foods/drinks containing various kinds of sugar (e.g. glucose syrup) only occasionally. Use herbs and spices as well as a little salt creatively. Prefer salt containing iodine.

Plenty of Liquids
Water is absolutely essential. Drink 1-2 l liquids every day. Prefer water (with or without gas) and other low-calorie drinks. Alcoholic drinks should not be taken.

Tasty Dishes, carefully cooked
Cook the meals with as low temperatures and as short as possible, using little water and fat – this preserves the original taste, keeps the nutrients intact and prevents the production of harmful compounds.

Take time and enjoy the food
Take your Time and enjoy your Food
Eating consciously helps to eat right. The eye enjoys food, too. It's fun, invites to enjoy varied dishes and stimulates the feeling of satiety.

Watch your Weight and stay in Motion
A balanced diet and a lot of exercise and sport (30 – 60 min/day) are a healthy combination. The right weight furthers well-being and health. Thermals, directional effectiveness, digestive power

There are various criteria for judging the effectiveness of herbs and foodstuffs.

The use of certain herbs and ingredients is based on observations of the effects on the body which these foodstuffs, herbs and spices show after having eaten them. The medical science has developed following system: Every ingredient or herb has a directional effectiveness. Furthermore, there are herbs which have a special effect on certain organs.

The basic condition for a healthy metabolism is to obtain sufficient energy from food and that the digestive process doesn't use too much energy. An easily digestible meal makes content and sated, doesn't cause flatulence and fatigue after the meal. The perfect spices increase the healthiness of our meals. Very often, just small doses of herbs and spices will suffice. They are not used to make us sated, but to help our digestive organs to digest the food.

12.2 Recipes

The recipes list the ingredients to be used and the cooking instructions show how the dish is prepared. The list of ingredients shows the concerned quantities as well as the relevance for the therapy. If you find „less than mentioned", try to comply or find an alternative from the „list of recommended foodstuffs". Mostly it shall result just in a small change of taste when you simply avoid this ingredient.

Mild cooking methods: boiling, stewing, poaching, steaming
Strong cooking methods: barbecuing, roasting, frying, smoking
Balanced cooking methods: deep-frying, baking brick
Deep-freezing and warming in the microwave oven should be avoided (denaturalization).

12.3 Foodstuffs

Foodstuffs have an effect on body and soul like medicinal herbs, only a very much milder one. Dietary advice is mainly based on regional foodstuffs. The knowledge about the effects of each foodstuff and the knowledge, when which foodstuff shall be used, is based on the orthodoschool of medicine. Use ecologic-organic products, if possible. As everything should be cooked for a long time due to a better digestability and very rarely eaten raw, the food agrees with everyone.

The classification of the foodstuffs according to their effect on the body is the basis in order to achieve a harmonious status of health.

Dietary advisors do not recommend certain foodstuffs for everyone. The individual diet is tailor-made for the individual constitution.

Buy only fresh and ripe fruit and vegetables. You ought to leave unripe fruit and vegetables and such with brown spots and wilted leaves behind in the market. In this case take deep-frozen goods (never ready-to-serve dishes!). Fruit and vegetables are deep-frozen immediately after harvesting and often contain more vitamins and minerals than the goods from the vegetable shelf. Whereas conserved or tinned goods contain very much less biological substances. Also, salt, sugar and others are mostly added to the latter. Never leave the foodstuffs in the water after washing them to avoid that many vital substances get drowned. Clean salads, fruit and vegetables immediately before serving.

Please make sure of the hygienic processing of foodstuffs. Clean your salads, fruit and vegetables carefully. When cooking with meat, prepare all ingredients first and then process the meat products. Clean the worktop and tools very carefully. Wooden surfaces ought to be treated with a mild disinfectant regularly in order to reduce germination. Store fruit and vegetables separately, if possible. Harvested fruit and vegetables are still alive and emit e.g. ethylene gas, which makes other products ripen and age faster. Keep meat and fish in the closed packaging or store them in the fridge in closed containers.

12.4 Herbs

There are some basic rules for storing medicinal herbs. On principle, herbs must be protected from direct sunlight, humidity and heat.

Containers for the storage of herbs may be glasses, ceramic jars and even plastic containers. However, plastic is a rather unsuitable material and should only be a short-term solution. In case of glass containers, use a dark material.

Medicinal herbs cannot be kept for any long period. The shelf life of herbs is limited. However, it can be prolonged with suitable storage. The place should be dark, rather cool and absolutely dry. A wooden medicine cabinet, placed not directly next to a source of heat, would be ideal. Never buy large quantities of herbs so as not to have to throw them away. Label the container with the name of the herb and the date of harvesting or processing.

13 Other dietic-books

The following syndromes of dietetics, TCM or for a therapy supplement for cancer are available.

Dietetics

E001. Nutrition of the infant - baby food
E002. Nutrition during lactation
E003. Nutrition in old age
E004. Nutrition of children and adolescents
E005. Nutrition of athletes
E006. Light weight
E007. Pregnancy
E008. Full food

Protein and electrolyte - kidneys
E009. (hemodialysis) dialysis treatment
E010. Acute renal failure
E011. Chronic renal insufficiency
E012. Nephrotic syndrome
E013. Kidney stones (nephrolithiasis)

Gastrointestinal tract - pancreas
E014. Acute pancreatitis (inflammation of the pancreas)
E015. Chronic pancreatitis (inflammation of the pancreas)

Gastrointestinal tract - small intestine and large intestine
E016. Acute obstipation (constipation)
E017. Chronic obstipation (constipation)
E018. Colon irritabile
E019. Diverticulitis
E020. Acquired lactose intolerance (lactose malabsorption)
E021. Fructose malabsorption
E022. Glutensensitive enteropathy (celiac disease)
E023. Colectomy
E024. Short Bowel Syndrome

Gastrointestinal tract - liver, gallbladder, bile ducts
E025. Acute and chronic hepatitis (inflammation of the liver)
E026. Cholelithiasis (bile stones)
E027. fatty liver
E028. cirrhosis

Gastrointestinal tract - Stomach and duodenal intestine
E029. Acute gastritis
E030. Chronic gastritis
E031. Stomach bleeding
E032. Ulcus ventriculi and duodenal ulcer
E033. Condition after gastric surgery

Gastrointestinal tract - oral cavity and esophagus
E034. Stomatitis
E035. Esophageal carcinoma (esophageal cancer)
E036. Refluosophagitis (heartburn)

Special diseases
E037. Phenylketonuria (PKU)
E038. Rheumatic joint diseases

Metabolism
E039. Obesity (overweight)
E040. Diabetes mellitus
E041. Eating disorders (underweight)

Fat metabolism
E042. Hypercholesterolaemia (increased cholesterol level)
E043. Hepatic Encephalopathy

Heart and circulation
E044. Arteriosclerosis (arterial calcification)
E045. Heart insufficiency
E046. Hypertension
E047. Hyperuricaemia and gout

Changed nutrient requirements
E048. In case of fever
E049. For malignant diseases
E050. After burns
E051. Radiation and chemotherapy

CANCER
E100. Pancreatic cancer
E101. Bladder cancer
E102. Blood cancer (leukemia)
E103. Breast cancer
E104. Colorectal cancer
E105. Gastric cancer
E106. Kidney cancer
E107. Esophageal cancer

TCM
E200. Bladder - moisture heat in the bladder
E201. Bladder - moisture and cold in the bladder
E202. Bladder - emptiness and cold in the bladder
E203. Large intestine - external cold affects the large intestine
E204. Large intestine - moisture heat in the large intestine
E205. Large intestine - heat blocks the intestine II acute
E206. Large intestine - dryness of the colon
E207. Large intestine - Yang deficiency (cold)
E208. Heart - Blood insufficiency
E209. Heart - Blood stagnation
E210. Heart - Fire
E211. Heart - Hot mucus clogs the heart pores
E212. Heart - Cold mucus clogs the heart pores
E213. Heart - Qi deficiency
E214. Heart - Yang deficiency
E215. Heart - Yin deficiency

E216. Liver - Ascending Liver Yang
E217. Liver - Blood deficiency
E218. Liver - Blood stagnation
E219. Liver - Moisture heat in liver and gall bladder
E220. Liver - Fire
E221. Liver - Gall bladder Qi-Empty
E222. Liver - Cold in the liver meridian
E223. Liver - Qi stagnation
E224. Liver - Wind
E225. Liver - Wind with ascending liver Yang
E226. Liver - Wind with blood anemic
E227. Liver - Wind with extreme heat
E228. Lung - Qi deficiency
E229. Lung - Mucus-moisture in the lungs
E230. Lung - Mucus-heat in the lungs
E231. Lung - Mucus-cold in the lungs
E232. Lung - Dryness of the lungs
E233. Lung - Wind-heat attacks the lungs
E234. Lung - Wind-cold affects the lungs
E235. Lung - Yin deficiency
E236. Stomach - Bloodstagnation
E237. Stomach - Fire
E238. Stomach - Cold with liquid
E239. Stomach - Nutrition stagnation
E240. Stomach - Qi deficiency
E241. Stomach - Rebellious Qi
E242. Stomach - Yin Emptiness
E243. Spleen - Heat and moisture attack the spleen
E244. Spleen - Coldness and moisture affects the spleen
E245. Spleen - Qi deficiency
E246. Spleen - Qi deficiency + Declining spleen Qi
E247. Spleen - Qi deficiency + spleen does not control the blood
E248. Spleen - Yang deficiency
E249. Kidney - Heart and kidney no longer communicate
E250. Kidney - Jing deficiency
E251. Kidney - Kidneys cannot receive the Qi
E252. Kidney - Qi is not stable
E253. Kidney - Yang deficiency
E254. Kidney - Yin deficiency

For further information visit nutribook.info.

14 EBNS - Software for nutritional counseling

The main task of the database is to create personalized nutritional advice for each patient individually. The database was developed for Dietetics and Traditional Chinese Medicine.
The Database supports training and advices in the daily work routine.

The computer program provides lists of recipes, ingredients and herbs, which are given to the client. individually adjustable according to patient's request from whole food to vegetarians (lacto, ovo, ...). For every register there is an information sheet which can be given to the client. All texts can be individually designed.

The syndromes can be combined and result in an intersection of the recommended recipes and ingredients. The automated diagnosis for the TCM enables you to check your experience during the training as well as to confirm your diagnosis in the working day. You select several predefined symptoms and have the program automatically display the relevant syndromes.

How to work with the database:
Select the patient / client, select one or more of the syndromes you diagnosed and print the folder.

You can change all values, create new symptoms or syndromes, develop recipes, change or adapt ingredients and herbs to your findings. In simple client management, all relevant data about the person is stored. You get an overview of the past diagnoses and the development of the course of the disease.

As a consultant you save a lot of time when you print out the recipe, food and herbal lists for the recognized syndromes and give them to the clients. You can use this time for a personal conversation. With the database, dieticians and nutritionists can view the nutrients and trace elements for each recipe and develop recipes for syndromes even with suggested ingredients.

All recipe and grocery lists can also be ordered from me as a combination of several diseases. I wish all readers good luck, health and happiness in life.
More information can be found at www.ebns.at.
Volunteer: www.krebsinfo.at
Josef Miligui